Non-Fiction Common Core Readings

Independence and Slavery

Thomas Jefferson: Views on Slavery and Framing Independence

Curriculum by
Elizabeth Chapin-Pinotti

Copyright © Lucky Willy Publishing, Inc.

ISBN: 978-0615850948

Table of Contents

Interpreting a Source Document Instructions   page 7

Declaration of Independence Notes   page 8

Letter to Henry Lee   page 9-10

Thomas Jefferson   page 12

Annotated: Little Journeys To the Homes of the Great   page 13

Letter to John Randolph, August 25, 1775   page 23

Letter to John Randolph, November 29, 1775   page 26

Letter to Benjamin Franklin, August 13, 1777   page 28

Drafting the Declaration   page 30

Towards Independence   page 37

Annotated from Thomas Jefferson's Memoir, Correspondence and Miscellanies   page 37

Thomas Jefferson and Slavery   page 48

Acknowledgments   page 57

Notes on Answers   page 58

To Dad

Thanks for my love of history

Interpreting a Source Document

Source Documents: The history we study today comes from analyzing the past by way of primary sources. A primary source is a document or a physical object written or created during the time period being studied. Primary source documents include letters, maps, journals, photographs and drawings. Primary sources also include news film footage, autobiographies, poetry, novels, furniture, clothing and buildings. Examples of primary sources include:

- The Declaration of Independence
- The Constitution of the United States
- Plato's Republic
- A civil war cannon ball

A secondary source analyzes or interprets primary sources. Secondary sources are one or more steps removed from the event being studied. Secondary sources include textbooks, magazine articles, commentaries and interpretations. Examples of secondary sources include:

- Magazine articles
- History textbooks
- A book about the readings of Thomas Jefferson

Rules for Analyzing Source Documents

Time and Place Rule: The closer to the time and place of the historical event, the more reliable a source is deemed. From top to bottom are the most reliable sources:

- Direct traces of the event;
- Accounts of the event by firsthand observers and/or participants created at the time of the event;
- Accounts of the event by firsthand observers and/or participant; created after the event occurred, by firsthand observers and participants;
- Accounts of the event, created after the event occurred, by people who did not participate or witness the event, but who used interviews or evidence from the time of the event.;
- A letter or journal writing when the event occurred by the parties of the event.

Bias Rule: Historians assume that every source is biased. Each piece must be looked at carefully and critically. Everyone has an opinion, so the creator's point of view must be considered.

Questions to Think About When Analyzing Source Documents:

- Who created the source and why?
- Did the recorder have firsthand knowledge of the event? Or, did the recorder report what others saw and heard?
- Was the recorder a neutral party? What is the personal bias?
- Why was the source produced? Was it personal, like a diary or public, like a report?

- Did the recorder or author have a reason to be dishonest or was he or she trying to persuade someone?
- Was the information recorded during the event, immediately after the event, or after some time had passed? If time had passed, what was the gap?

Asking yourself these questions as you work through primary sources will help you analyze the source and make a determination. It may be easier, and even tempting, to use a textbook or the internet to help you interpret something that you may not completely understand, but a critical part of the learning process is to think for yourself and form your own opinions. Who knows? You may make some stellar historical breakthrough by thinking of something that no one has ever thought before.

Think of studying history and sorting through both primary and secondary sources as a great scavenger hunt where the prize at the end of the hunt is discovering, maybe even for the first time, what life was like in the past and what led up to major events in history!

Above is a copy of Jefferson's original notes for the Declaration of Independence. This copy is from The Library of Congress. It is the only known piece of the earliest draft of this important document. It is heavily edited. Looking at, studying and analyzing this fragment would be working with a primary source document.

On the next two pages is an example of a primary source document. It is a letter written by Thomas Jefferson, who, as he grew older, became more and more concerned that people understand the principles underlying the writing and adoption of the Declaration of Independence.

In the following letter, Jefferson wrote: "this was the object of the Declaration of Independence. not to find out new principles, or new arguments, never before thought of, not merely to say things which had never been said before; but to place before mankind the common sense of the subject, in terms so plain and firm as to command their assent, and to justify ourselves in the independent stand we [were] compelled to take."

Dear Sir   Monticello May 8. 25.   322

     Your favor of Apr. 29 has been duly recieved, and the offer of mineralogical specimens from mr Meyer has been communicated to Dr. Emmet our Professor of Natural history. the last donation of the legislature to the University, was appropriated specifically to a library and apparatus of every kind. but we apply it first to the more important articles of a library, of an astronomical, physical, & chemical apparatus. and we think it safest to see what these will cost, before we venture on collections of mineral & other subjects. the last we must proportion to what we shall have left only. the Professor possesses already what he thinks will be sufficient for mineralogical and geological explanations to his school. I do not know how far he might be tempted to enlarge his possession by a catalogue of the articles and prices, if both should be satisfactory. if mr Meyer chuses to send such a catalogue, it shall be returned to you immediately, if the purchase be not approved.

    That George Mason was author of the bill of rights, and of the constitution founded on it, the evidence of the day established fully in my mind. of the paper you mention, purporting to be instructions to the Virginia delegation in Congress, I have no recollection. if it were any thing more than a projet of some private hand, that is to say, had any such instructions been ever given by the Convention, they would appear in the Journals, which we possess entire. but with respect to our rights and the acts of the British government contravening those rights, there was but one opinion on this side of the water. all american whigs thought alike on these subjects. when forced therefore to resort to arms for redress, an appeal to the tribunal of the world was deemed proper for our justification. this was the object of the Declaration of Independance. not to find out new principles, or new arguments, never before thought of, not merely to say things which had never been said before; but to place before mankind the common sense of the subject; in terms so plain and firm as to command their assent, and to justify ourselves in the independant stand we are compelled to take. neither aiming at originality of principle or sentiment, nor yet copied from any particular and previous writing, it was intended to be an expression of the american mind, and to give to that expression the proper tone and spirit called for by the occasion. all it's authority rests then on the harmonising sentiments of the day, whether expressed in conversation, in letters, printed essays or in the elementary books

40298   Henry Lee esq.

of public right, as Aristotle, Cicero, Locke, Sidney &c. the historical documents which you mention as in your possession, ought to be found, and I am persuaded you will find, to be corroborative of the facts and principles advanced in the Declaration. be pleased to accept assurances of my great respect and esteem.

Th: Jefferson

Document Analysis

1. Type of Document: _____

2. Date of Document: _____ 3. Author of Document: _____

4. Title of the Document: _____

5. Who is the Document's Intended Audience: _____
_____
_____
_____

6. List three things the author said that you think are important:
_____
_____
_____

7. Why do you think the document was written:
_____
_____
_____

8. What is the evidence that helps you understand why it was written:
_____
_____
_____

9. List two things the document tells you about life in the United States at the time it was written:
_____
_____
_____

10. Write a question to the author that is left unanswered by the document:
_____
_____
_____

Thomas Jefferson

This *Thomas Jefferson* chapter contains source documents and important writings by and about Thomas Jefferson. When studying history, it is important to remember that our founding fathers were real people, with homes and families and hopes and dreams…and ideals. Try to keep that in mind as you read their words.

Excerpts from:

i.   Little Journeys To the Homes of the Great, *Volume 3, Little Journeys To The Homes Of American Statesmen* by Elbert Hubbard. Originally published in 1916.

ii. Memoir, Correspondence and Miscellanies: From the Papers of Thomas Jefferson, edited by Thomas Jefferson Randolph (1829).

iii. Various letters and documents written by Thomas Jefferson annotated.

Original spelling, punctuation and grammar left intact.

As you read:

- Think about the philosophy of the government expressed in the following writings by Thomas Jefferson.
- Think about the emphasis of securing individual rights.
- Analyze what "all men are created equal" really means.

Thomas Jefferson and the Founding of the United States of America

From: <u>Little Journeys To the Homes of the Great</u>, *Volume 3, Little Journeys To The Homes Of American Statesmen* by Elbert Hubbard. Originally published in 1916.

THOMAS JEFFERSON

William and Mary College was founded in Sixteen Hundred Ninety-two by the persons whose names it bears. The founders bestowed on it an **endowment** that would have been generous had there not been attached to it sundry strings in way of conditions.

The intent was to make Indians Episcopalians, and white students clergymen; and the assumption being that between the whites and the **aborigines** there was little difference, the curriculum was an ecclesiastic medley.

All the teachers were appointed by the Bishop of London, and the places were usually given to clergymen who were not needed in England.

To this college, in Seventeen Hundred Sixty, came Thomas Jefferson, a tall, red-haired youth, aged seventeen. He had a sharp nose and a sharp chin; and a youth having these has a sharp intellect—mark it well.

This boy had not been "sent" to college. He came of his own accord from his home at Shadwell, five days' horseback journey through the woods. His father was dead, and his mother, a rare gentle soul, was an invalid.

Death is not a calamity "per se," nor is physical weakness necessarily a curse, for out of these seeming unkind conditions Nature often distils her finest products. The dying injunction of a father may impress itself upon a son as no example of right living ever can, and the physical disability of a mother may be the means that work for excellence and strength. The last-expressed wish of Peter Jefferson was that his son should be well educated, and attain to a degree of useful manliness that the father had never reached. And into the keeping of this fourteen-year-old youth the dying man, with the last flicker of his intellect, gave the mother, sisters and baby brother.

We often hear of persons who became aged in a single night, their hair turning from dark to white; but I have seen death thrust responsibility upon a lad and make of him a man between the rising of the sun and its setting. When we talk of "right environment" and the "proper conditions" that should surround growing youth, we fan the air with words—there is no such thing as a universal right environment.

Thomas Jefferson	
Physical Features	
Intellect	
Family	

Use the space below to summarize the passage below:

_____

_____

_____

_____

_____

_____

_____

_____

_____

_____

_____

_____

_____

_____

_____

_____

Activity 2:

Think and Write: William and Mary is a college in Williamsburg, Virginia. It is the second oldest college in the United States. Thomas Jefferson began William and Mary in March of 1760 at the age of sixteen. During his first two years at the college, Jefferson lived in the Sir Christopher Wren Building. The Wren Building, as it is called today, is still used. The building is alive with classrooms and meeting halls and active students.

The Wren Building at William and Mary with Thomas Jefferson Statue. Picture Steven James.

During his college years, Jefferson studied philosophy – which included physics, metaphysics and mathematics. He also studied moral philosophy – which included rhetoric, logic and ethics. Jefferson was a diligent student who often studied fifteen hours a day. He then studied law, also at William and Mary.

Evidence of Jefferson's maturing ideas of freedom and self-government surfaced in Williamsburg during these years. As a law student, he stood enraptured at the doorway of the House of Burgesses, listening to Patrick Henry speak out against the Stamp Act. As a burgess, Jefferson continued to promote the idea of revolution. As a lawyer, he practiced at the General Court. In 1770, he defended a slave. Despite owning slaves all his life, he spoke then against slavery, saying under the law of nature, "we are all born free."

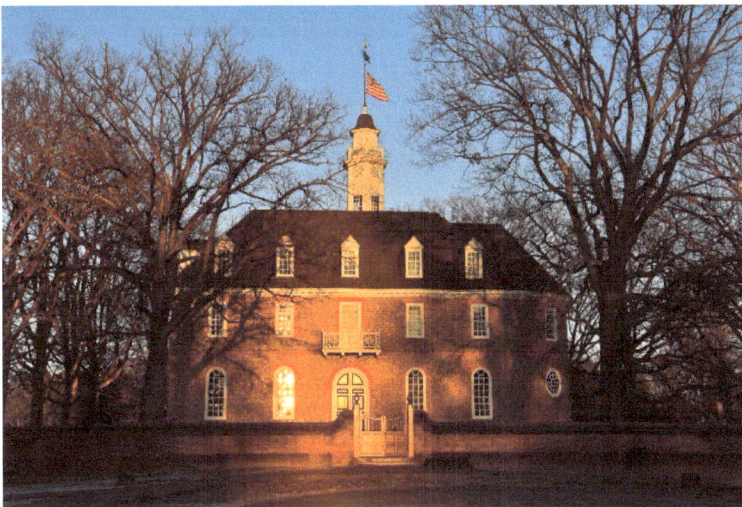

Virginia House of Burgesses

Williamsburg, and William and Mary, became an early hub for our founding fathers. Just down the street from the college is the Virginia House of Burgesses where Jefferson eventually worked with George Washington, Patrick Henry and others as they prepared to declare independence from the British government and begin the United States of America.

Williamsburg was the thriving capital of Virginia when the dream of American freedom and independence was taking shape. For 81 formative years, from 1699 to 1780, Williamsburg was the political, cultural, and educational center of what was then the largest, most populous, and most influential of the American colonies. It was here that the fundamental concepts of our republic — responsible leadership, a sense of public service, self-government, and individual liberty — were nurtured under the leadership of patriots such as George Washington, Thomas Jefferson, George Mason, and Peyton Randolph.

Think about the statement: *"as a student at William and Mary, young Jefferson had the ideal place from which to observe and be taught as he prepared to help form a new nation."*
Do you agree or disagree? Please support your answer.

I _____, because _____
_____
_____
_____
_____
_____
_____
_____
_____
_____
_____
_____
_____
_____
_____
_____
_____
_____
_____
_____
_____

Think about the statement: *"Doctor Small encouraged the young farmer from the hills to think and to express himself"*. What does that statement mean to you: _____

_____

_____

_____

_____

_____

_____

Remember: You have thoughts and ideas and studying history is about looking at what happened in the past and forming your own ideas based on evidence. It is also about looking at situations and thinking about how what happened shaped the future.

What do you know about Thomas Jefferson?

_____

_____

_____

_____

_____

_____

_____

_____

_____

_____

Back to the Passage: THOMAS JEFFERSON:

Williamsburg was then the capital of Virginia. It contained only about a thousand inhabitants, but when the Legislature was in session it was very gay.

At one end of a wide avenue was the Capitol, and at the other the Governor's "palace"; and when the city of Washington was laid out, Williamsburg served as a model. On Saturdays, there were horse-races on the "Avenue"; everybody gambled; cockfights and dogfights were regarded as manly diversions; there was much **carousing** at taverns; and often at private houses there were all-night dances where the rising sun found everybody but the servant's plain drunk.

At the college, both teachers and scholars were obliged to subscribe to the Thirty-nine Articles and to recite the Catechism[1]. The atmosphere was charged with theology.

Young Jefferson had never before seen a village of even a dozen houses, and he looked upon this as a type of all cities. He thought about it, talked about it, wrote about it, and we now know that at this time his ideas concerning city versus country crystallized.

Fifty years after, when he had come to know London and Paris, and had seen the chief cities of Christendom, he repeated the words he had written in youth, "The hope of a nation lies in its tillers of the soil!"

On his mother's side he was related to the "first families," but aristocracy and caste had no fascination for him, *and he then began forming those ideas of utility, simplicity and equality that time only strengthened.*

His tutors and professors served chiefly as "horrible examples," with the shining exception of Doctor Small. The friendship that ripened between this man and young Jefferson is an ideal example of what can be done through the personal touch. Men are great only as they excel in sympathy; and the difference between sympathy and imagination has not yet been shown us.

---

[1] The "Thirty-Nine" Articles of Religion refer to the statement of doctrines of the Church of England.

Doctor Small encouraged the young farmer from the hills to think and to express himself. He did not endeavor to set him straight or explain everything for him, or correct all his vagaries or demand that he should memorize rules. He gave his affectionate sympathy to the boy.

To Doctor Small, pedigree and history unknown, let us give the credit of being first in the list of friends that gave bent to the mind of Jefferson. John Burke, in his "History of Virginia," refers to Professor Small thus: "He was not any too orthodox in his opinions." And here we catch a glimpse of a formative influence in the life of Jefferson that caused him to turn from the letter of the law and cleave to the spirit that maketh alive. After school-hours the tutor and the student walked and talked, and on Saturdays and Sundays went on excursions through the woods; and to the youth there was given an impulse for a scientific knowledge of birds and flowers and the host of life that thronged the forest. And when the pair had strayed so far beyond the town that darkness gathered and the stars came out, they conversed of the wonders of the sky.

The true scientist has no passion for killing things. He says with Thoreau, "To shoot a bird is to lose it." Professor Small had the gentle instinct that respects life, and he refused to take that which he could not give. *To his youthful companion he imparted, in a degree, the secret of enjoying things without the passion for possession and the lust of ownership.*

There is a myth abroad that college towns are intellectual centers; but the number of people in a college town (or any other) who really think, is very few.

Williamsburg was gay, and, this much said, it is needless to add it was not intellectual. But Professor Small was a thinker, and so was Governor Fauquier; and these two were firm friends, although very unlike in many ways. And to "the palace" of the courtly Fauquier, Small took his young friend Jefferson. Fauquier was often a master of the revels, but after his seasons of dissipation he turned to Small for absolution and comfort. At these times he seemed to Jefferson a paragon of excellence. To the grace of the French he added the earnestness of the English. He quoted Pope, and talked of Swift, Addison and Thomson. Fauquier and Jefferson became friends, although more than a score of years and a world of experience separated them. Jefferson caught a little of Fauquier's grace, love of books and delight in architecture. But Fauquier helped him most by gambling away all his ready

Think about the following quote in relation to what you know about the **Declaration of Independence** *"To his youthful companion he imparted, in a degree, the secret of enjoying things without the passion for possession and the lust of ownership."*

_____
_____
_____
_____
_____
_____
_____
_____
_____
_____
_____
_____
_____
_____
_____
_____
_____
_____
_____
_____
_____
_____

Why do you think Patrick Henry and Thomas Jefferson became friends: _____

_____

_____

_____

_____

_____

_____

_____

Compare and Contrast: To be a lawyer in the United States today, students need to go to four years of college or university to get a Bachelor's degree and then go to three more years of law school. Using the article as your source, what do you think was needed to be an attorney in the days of Thomas Jefferson?

_____

_____

_____

_____

_____

_____

_____

_____

After Patrick Henry passed the bar exam, what did he do?_____

_____

_____

_____

_____

_____

_____

_____

_____

money and getting drunk and smoking strong pipes with his feet on the table. And Jefferson then vowed he would never handle a card, nor use tobacco, nor drink intoxicating liquors. And in conversation with Small, he anticipated Buckle by saying, "To gain leisure, wealth must first be secured; but once leisure is gained, more people use it in the pursuit of pleasure than employ it in acquiring knowledge."

About this time the rollicking Patrick Henry came along. Patrick played the violin, and so did Thomas. These two young men had first met on a musical basis. Some otherwise sensible people hold that musicians are shallow and impractical; and I know one man who declares that truth and honesty and uprightness never dwelt in a professional musician's heart; and further, that the tribe is totally incapable of comprehending the difference between "meum" and "tuum." But then this same man claims that actors are rascals who have lost their own characters in the business of playing they are somebody else. And yet I'll explain for the benefit of the captious that, although Thomas Jefferson and Patrick Henry both fiddled, they never did and never would fiddle while Rome burned. Music was with them a pastime, not a profession.

As soon as Patrick Henry arrived at Williamsburg, he sought out his old friend Thomas Jefferson, because he liked him—and to save tavern bill. And Patrick announced that he had come to Williamsburg to be admitted to the bar.

"How long have you studied law?" asked Jefferson.

"Oh, for six weeks last Tuesday," was the answer.

Tradition has it that Jefferson advised Patrick to go home and study at least a fortnight more before making his application. But Patrick declared that the way to learn law is to practice it, and he surely was right. Most young lawyers are really never aware of how little law they know until they begin to practice.

But Patrick Henry was duly admitted, although George Wythe protested. Then Patrick went back home to tend bar (the other kind) for Laban, his father-in-law, for full four years. He studied hard and practiced a little betimes— and his is the only instance that history records of a barkeeper acquiring wisdom while following his calling; but for the encouragement of youth I write it down.

No doubt it was the example of Patrick Henry that caused Jefferson to adopt his profession. But it was the literary side of law that first attracted him—not the practice of it. As a speaker he was singularly deficient, a slight physical malformation of the throat giving him a very poor and uncertain voice. But he studied law, and after all it does not make much difference what a man studies—**all knowledge is related, and the man who studies anything if he keeps at it will become learned....**

…When twenty-four, he hung out his lawyer's sign under that of George Wythe at Williamsburg. And clients came that way with retainers, and rich planters sent him business, and wealthy widows advised with him—and still he could not make a speech without stuttering. Many men can harangue a jury, and every village has its orator; but where is the wise and silent man who will advise you in a way that will keep you out of difficulty, protect your threatened interests, and conduct the affairs you may leave in his hands so as to return your ten talents with other talents added! And I hazard the statement, without heat or prejudice, that if the experiment should be made with a thousand lawyers in any one of our larger cities, four-fifths of them would be found so deficient, either mentally, morally or both, that if ten talents were placed in their hands, they would not at the close of a year be able to account for the principal, to say nothing of the interest. And the bar of today is made up of a better class than it was in Jefferson's time, even if it has not the intellectual fiber that it had forty years ago.

But at the early age of twenty-five, Jefferson was a wise and skilful man in the world's affairs (and a man who is wise is also honest), and men of this stamp do not remain hidden in obscurity. The world needs just such individuals and needs them badly. Jefferson had the quiet, methodical industry that works without undue expenditure of nervous force; that intuitive talent which enables the possessor to read a whole page at a glance and drop at once upon the vital point; and then he had the ability to get his whole case on paper, marshaling his facts in a brief, pointed way that served to convince better than eloquence. These are the characteristics that make for success in practice before our Courts of Appeal; and Jefferson's success shows that they serve better than bluster, even with a backwoods bench composed of fox-hunting farmers.

In Seventeen Hundred Sixty-eight, when Jefferson was twenty-five, he went down to Shadwell and ran for member of the Virginia Legislature. It was the proper thing to do, for he was the richest man in the county, being heir to his father's forty thousand acres, and it was expected that he would represent his district. He called on every voter in the parish, shook hands with everybody, complimented the ladies, caressed the babies, treated crowds at every tavern, and kept a large punch-bowl and open house at home. He was elected. On the Eleventh of May, Seventeen Hundred Sixty-nine, the Legislature convened, with nearly a hundred members present, Colonel George Washington being one of the number. It took two days for the Assembly to elect a Speaker and get ready for business. On the third day, four resolutions were introduced—pushed to the front largely through the influence of our new member.

These resolutions were:

1. No taxation without representation.
2. The Colonies may concur and unite in seeking redress for grievances.
3. Sending accused persons away from their own country for trial is an inexcusable wrong.
4. We will send an address on these things to the King beseeching his royal interposition.

The resolutions were passed: they did not mean much anyway, the opposition said. And then another resolution was passed to this effect: "We will send a copy of these resolutions to every legislative body on the continent." That was a little stronger, but did not mean much either.

It was voted upon and passed.

Then the Assembly adjourned, having dispatched a copy of the resolutions to Lord Boutetourt, the newly appointed Governor who had just arrived from London.

Next day, the Governor's secretary appeared when the Assembly convened, and repeated the following formula: "The Governor commands the House to attend His Excellency in the Council-Chamber." The members marched to the Council-Chamber and stood around the throne waiting the pleasure of His Lordship. He made a speech which I will quote entire. "Mr. Speaker and Gentlemen of the House of Burgesses: I have heard your resolves, and augur ill of their effect. You have made it my duty to dissolve you, and you are dissolved accordingly."

And that was the end of Jefferson's first term in office—the reward for all the hand-shaking, all the caressing, all the treating!

The members looked at one another, but no one said anything, because there was nothing to say. The secretary made an impatient gesture with his hand to the effect that they should disperse, and they did.

Just how these legally elected representatives and now legally common citizens took their rebuff we do not know.

Did Washington forget his usual poise and break out into one of those swearing fits where everybody wisely made way? And how did Richard Henry Lee like it, and George Wythe, and the Randolphs? Did Patrick Henry wax eloquent that afternoon in a barroom, and did Jefferson do more than smile grimly, biding his time?

Massachusetts kept a complete history of her political heresies, but Virginia chased foxes and left the refinements of literature to dilettantes. But this much we know: Those country gentlemen did not go off peaceably and quietly to race horses or play cards. The slap in the face from the gloved hand of Lord Boutetourt awoke every boozy sense of security and gave vitality to all fanatical messages sent by Samuel Adams. Washington, we are told, spoke of it as a bit of upstart authority on the part of the new Governor; but Jefferson with true prophetic vision saw the end.

What do you notice about the picture at right? _____
_____
_____
_____
_____
_____
_____
_____
_____
_____
_____
_____
_____
_____
_____
_____

Activity: Colonists Treatment by the British Government

Here are the facts:

- The British Government called for the colonies to elect officials to serve as representatives.
- In Virginia those representatives served in the House of Burgesses or legislature.
- The British Government was in debt over the Seven Years War.
- The British Government needed money.
- The British Government taxed and taxed and taxed the colonies.
- The representatives of the Virginia House of Burgesses, or legislature, passed resolutions against unfair acts – including those taxes.
- The British Government did not like the resolutions.
- The British Government dissolved the elected legislature because it didn't like what they were doing.

Write and Think: Write a paragraph regarding the reasons the Virginia House of Burgesses passed the following resolutions:

1. No taxation without representation.
2. The Colonies may concur and unite in seeking redress for grievances.
3. Sending accused persons away from their own country for trial is an inexcusable wrong.
4. We will send an address on these things to the King beseeching his royal interposition.

Discuss whether you think the fact that the British Government dissolved the Virginia House of Burgesses after they expressed their opinion was appropriate. Support your claims with logical reasoning and relevant, accurate data from the text.

_____

_____

_____

_____

_____

_____

_____

_____

_____

_____

_____

_____

_____

TO JOHN RANDOLPH, August 25, 1775

TO JOHN RANDOLPH, ESQ.,

Monticello,

August 25, 1775.

Dear Sir,

I am sorry the situation of our country should render it not eligible to you to remain longer in it. I hope the returning wisdom of Great Britain will, ere long, put an end to this unnatural contest. There may be people to whose tempers and dispositions contention is pleasing, and who, therefore, wish a continuance of confusion; but to me it is of all states but one, the most horrid: My first wish is a restoration of our just rights; my second, a return of the happy period, when, consistently with duty, I may withdraw myself totally from the public stage, and pass the rest of my days in domestic ease and tranquillity, banishing every desire of ever hearing what passes in the world. Perhaps, (for the latter adds considerably to the warmth of the former wish,) looking with fondness towards a reconciliation with Great Britain, I cannot help hoping you may be able to contribute towards expediting this good work. I think it must be evident to yourself, that the Ministry have been deceived by their officers on this side of the water, who (for what purpose, I cannot tell) have constantly represented the American opposition as that of a small faction, in which the body of the people took little part. This, you can inform them, of your own knowledge, is untrue. They have taken it into their heads, too, that we are cowards, and shall surrender at discretion to an armed force. The past and future operations of the war must confirm or undeceive them on that head. I wish they were thoroughly and minutely acquainted with every circumstance relative to America, as it exists in truth. I am persuaded, this would go far towards disposing them to reconciliation. Even those in Parliament who are called friends to America, seem to know nothing of our real determinations. I observe, they pronounced in the last Parliament, that the Congress of 1774 did not mean to insist rigorously on the terms they held out, but kept something in reserve, to give up: and, in fact, that they would give up every thing but the article of taxation. Now, the truth is far from this, as I can affirm, and put my honor to the assertion. Their continuance in this error may perhaps produce very ill consequences. The Congress stated the lowest terms they thought possible to be accepted, in order to convince the world they were not unreasonable. They gave up the monopoly and regulation of trade, and all acts of Parliament prior to 1764, leaving to British generosity to render these, at some future time, as easy to America as the interest of Britain would admit. But this was before blood was spilt. I cannot affirm, but have reason to think, these terms would not now be accepted. I wish no false sense of honor, no ignorance of our real intentions, no vain hope that partial concessions of right will be accepted, may induce the Ministry to trifle with accommodation, till it shall be out of their power ever to accommodate. If, indeed, Great Britain, disjoined from her colonies, be a match for the most potent nations of Europe, with the colonies thrown into their scale, they may go on securely. But if they are not assured of this, it would be certainly unwise, by trying the event of another campaign, to risk our accepting a foreign aid, which perhaps may not be obtainable but on condition of everlasting avulsion from Great Britain. This would be thought a hard condition to those who still wish for reunion with their parent country. I am sincerely one of those, and would rather be in dependence on Great Britain, properly limited, than on any nation upon earth, or than on no nation. But I am one of those, too, who, rather than submit to the rights of legislating for us, assumed by the British Parliament, and which late experience has shown they will so cruelly exercise, would lend my hand to sink the whole island in the ocean.

If undeceiving the Minister, as to matters of fact, may change his disposition, it will perhaps be in your power, by assisting to do this, to render service to the whole empire at the most critical time, certainly, that it has ever seen. Whether Britain shall continue the head of the greatest empire on earth, or shall return to her original station in the political scale of Europe, depends perhaps on the resolutions of the succeeding winter. God send they may be wise and salutary for us all. I shall be glad to hear from you as often as you may be disposed to think of things here. You may be at liberty, I expect; to communicate some things, consistently with your honor and the duties you will owe to a protecting nation. Such a communication among individuals may be mutually beneficial to the contending parties. On this or any future occasion, if I affirm to you any facts, your knowledge of me will enable you to decide on their credibility; if I hazard opinions on the dispositions of men or other speculative points, you can only know they are my opinions. My best wishes for your felicity attend you wherever you go; and believe me to be, assuredly,

Your friend and servant,

Th: Jefferson.

Document Analysis: Letter to John Randolph, August 25, 1775

1. Type of Document: _____

2. Date of Document: _____ 3. Author of Document: _____

4. Title of the Document: _____

5. Who is the Document's Intended Audience: _____

_____

_____

_____

6. List three things the author said that you think are important:

_____

_____

_____

7. Why do you think the document was written:

_____

_____

_____

8. What is the evidence that helps you understand why it was written:

_____

_____

_____

9. List two things the document tells you about life in the United States at the time it was written:

_____

_____

_____

10. Write a question to the author that is left unanswered by the document:

_____

_____

_____

TO JOHN RANDOLPH, November 29, 1775

TO JOHN RANDOLPH, ESQ.

Philadelphia,

November 29, 1775.

Dear Sir,

I am to give you the melancholy intelligence of the death of our most worthy Speaker, which happened here on the 22nd of the last month. He was struck with an apoplexy, and expired within five hours.

I have it in my power to acquaint you that the success of our arms has corresponded with the justness of our cause. Chambly and St. Johns were taken some weeks ago, and in them the whole regular army in Canada, except about forty or fifty men. This day certain intelligence has reached us that our General, Montgomery, is received into Montreal: and we expect every hour to be informed that Quebec has opened its arms to Colonel Arnold, who, with eleven hundred men, was sent from Boston up the Kennebec, and down the Chaudiere river to that place. He expected to be there early this month. Montreal acceded to us on the 13th, and Carleton set out, with the shattered remains of his little army, for Quebec, where we hope he will be taken up by Arnold. In a short time, we have reason to hope, the delegates of Canada will join us in Congress, and complete the American union as far as we wish to have it completed. We hear that one of the British transports has arrived at Boston; the rest are beating off the coast, in very bad weather. You will have heard, before this reaches you, that Lord Dunmore has commenced hostilities in Virginia. That people bore with every thing, till he attempted to burn the town of Hampton. They opposed and repelled him, with considerable loss on his side, and none on ours. It has raised our countrymen into a perfect phrenzy. It is an immense misfortune to the whole empire to have a King of such a disposition at such a time. We are told, and every thing proves it true, that he is the bitterest enemy we have. His Minister is able, and that satisfies me that ignorance, or wickedness, somewhere, controls him. In an earlier part of this contest, our petitions told him, that from our King there was but one appeal. The admonition was despised, and that appeal forced on us. To undo his empire, he has but one truth more to learn; that, after colonies have drawn the sword, there is but one step more they can take. That step is now pressed upon us by the measures adopted, as if they were afraid we would not take it. Believe me, dear Sir, there is not in the British empire a man who more cordially loves a union with Great Britain than I do. But, by the God that made me, I will cease to exist before I yield to a connection on such terms as the British Parliament propose; and in this, I think I speak the sentiments of America. We want neither inducement nor power to declare and assert a separation. It is will alone which is wanting, and that is growing apace under the fostering hand of our King. One bloody campaign will probably decide everlastingly our future course; I am sorry to find a bloody campaign is decided on. If our winds and waters should not combine to rescue their shores from slavery, and General Howe's reinforcement should arrive in safety, we have hopes he will be inspirited to come out of Boston and take another drubbing: and we must drub him soundly before the sceptred tyrant will know we are not mere brutes, to crouch under his hand, and kiss the rod with which he deigns to scourge us.

Yours, &c.

Th: Jefferson.

Document Analysis: Letter to John Randolph, November 29, 1775

1. Type of Document: _____

2. Date of Document: _____ 3. Author of Document: _____

4. Title of the Document: _____

5. Who is the Document's Intended Audience: _____

_____

_____

_____

6. List three things the author said that you think are important:

_____

_____

_____

7. Why do you think the document was written:

_____

_____

_____

8. What is the evidence that helps you understand why it was written:

_____

_____

_____

9. List two things the document tells you about life in the United States at the time it was written:

_____

_____

_____

10. Write a question to the author that is left unanswered by the document:

_____

_____

_____

TO BENJAMIN FRANKLIN, August 13, 1777

TO DR. BENJAMIN FRANKLIN, PARIS.

Virginia, August 13, 1777.

Honorable Sir,

I forbear to write you news, as the time of Mr. Shore's departure being uncertain, it might be old before you receive it, and he can, in person, possess you of all we have. With respect to the State of Virginia in particular, the people seem to have laid aside the monarchical, and taken up the republican government, with as much ease as would have attended their throwing off an old and putting on a new suit of clothes. Not a single throe has attended this important transformation. A half dozen aristocratical gentlemen, agonizing under the loss of pre-eminence, have sometimes ventured their sarcasms on our political metamorphosis. They have been thought fitter objects of pity than of punishment. We are at present in the complete and quiet exercise of well organized government, save only that our courts of justice do not open till the fall. I think nothing can bring the security of our continent and its cause into danger, if we can support the credit of our paper. To do that, I apprehend one of two steps must be taken. Either to procure free trade by alliance with some naval power able to protect it; or, if we find there is no prospect of that, to shut our ports totally to all the world, and turn our colonies into manufactories. The former would be most eligible, because most conformable to the habits and wishes of our people. Were the British Court to return to their senses in time to seize the little advantage which still remains within their reach from this quarter, I judge that, on acknowledging our absolute independence and sovereignty, a commercial treaty beneficial to them, and perhaps even a league of mutual offence and defence, might, not seeing the expense or consequences of such a measure, be approved by our people, if nothing in the mean time, done on your part, should prevent it. But they will continue to grasp at their desperate sovereignty, till every benefit short of that is for ever out of their reach. I wish my domestic situation had rendered it possible for me to join you in the very honorable charge confided to you. Residence in a polite Court, society of literati of the first order, a just cause and an approving God, will add length to a life for which all men pray, and none more than

Your most obedient and humble servant,

Th: Jefferson.

Think and Write: How does this document tie in with the previous two letters from Thomas Jefferson to John Randolph? What is the thematic link?

_____
_____
_____
_____
_____
_____
_____
_____
_____
_____

Document Analysis: Letter to Benjamin Franklin 1777

1. Type of Document: _____

2. Date of Document: _____ 3. Author of Document: _____

4. Title of the Document: _____

5. Who is the Document's Intended Audience: _____
_____
_____
_____

6. List three things the author said that you think are important:
_____
_____
_____

7. Why do you think the document was written:
_____
_____
_____

8. What is the evidence that helps you understand why it was written:
_____
_____
_____

9. List two things the document tells you about life in the United States at the time it was written:
_____
_____
_____

10. Write a question to the author that is left unanswered by the document:
_____
_____
_____

Drafting the Declaration of Independence

Thomas Jefferson is responsible for writing the bulk of the Declaration of Independence. While George Washington and his army set off to battle the British, the Second Continental Congress met in Philadelphia to formalize matters at home. There wasn't yet a formal "federal" government. Each colony had its own legislature and there was no central authority to govern the very different and not at all unified country. In fact, most people disagreed about most things.

There was one thing they did agree on, however, and that was: the American colonies needed to declare, formally and unequivocally, their independence from King George III. They just didn't know exactly how to go about doing it. It was during this Second Continental Congress when a representative from Virginia, named Richard Henry Lee, submitted a resolution to choose a committee to prepare the Declaration of Independence. The date was June 11, 1776 and the committee numbered five: Thomas Jefferson of Virginia, Roger Sherman of Connecticut, Benjamin Franklin of Pennsylvania, Robert R. Livingston of New York and John Adams of Massachusetts. Thomas Jefferson prepared the first draft.

Jefferson was a scholar and drew much of the Declaration language from his studies of John Locke's theory of government. Jefferson completed a draft he was willing to share; however, the original draft included an indictment of the slave trade. While Jefferson owned slaves himself, he was conflicted about slavery. This "anti-slavery" passage was cut, because others on the committee feared its inclusion would cause some members of the Continental Congress to vote against the Declaration and this would be unacceptable.

The omitted indictment of the slave trade read: *"He* (Britain) *has waged cruel war against human nature itself, violating its most sacred rights of life & liberty in the persons of a distant people who never offended him, captivating & carrying them into slavery in another hemisphere, or to incur miserable death in their transportation thither."*

On July 1, 1776, the Continental Congress reconvened. On July 4, 1776, the Declaration of Independence was adopted. On July 9, all thirteen colonies approved the draft and the official document was signed.

The document is divided into five parts: the preamble, the body (which contains the Statement of Human Rights and the Charges against the King and Parliament) and the conclusion or Statement of Separation.

The Declaration of Independence puts forth that all men are created equal and are entitled to "life, liberty and the pursuit of happiness." These ideals, written so long ago, are the foundation upon which our government was built.

Think and Write: Re-read the omitted passage regarding the indictment of the slave trade and discuss why you feel it was omitted from the original document.

_____

_____

_____

_____

_____

_____   30

Activity: On the following pages is a copy of the original draft of the Declaration of Independence, with notes by Benjamin Franklin included. There are passages crossed out and words inserted, but if you look closely you will find that most of document was written in one attempt. Such an important document, and one so eloquently expressive of the ideals of our government, written almost entirely in one draft is amazing when you consider how much is expressed in the Declaration of Independence.

Please read the Declaration of Independence from the copies of the original draft on the next four pages and write a summary of what you consider the most important points.

Introductory Statement:
Most Important Point 1:
Supporting Detail:
Supporting Detail:
Supporting Detail:
Most Important Point 2:
Supporting Detail:
Supporting Detail:
Supporting Detail:
Most Important Point 3:
Supporting Detail:
Supporting Detail:
Supporting Detail:
Summarize Your Thoughts and Conclude:

Copy of Draft
Declaration of
Independence
from the U.S.
National
Archives.

A Declaration by the Representatives of the UNITED STATES OF AMERICA, in General Congress assembled.

When in the course of human events it becomes necessary for one people to dissolve the political bands which have connected them with another, and to ~~assume from that subordination~~ ~~in which they have hitherto remained, &~~] assume among the powers of the earth the separate and equal ~~equal & independent~~ station to which the laws of nature & of nature's god entitle them, a decent respect to the opinions of mankind requires that they should declare the causes which impel them to the ~~change~~ the separation

We hold these truths to be self-evident, ~~sacred & undeniable~~; that all men are created equal ~~& independent~~; that ~~from~~ that equal creation they derive ~~rights~~ ~~inherent & inalienable~~, among ~~which~~ these are ~~the preservation of~~ life & liberty, & the pursuit of happiness; that to secure these rights, go-vernments are instituted among men, deriving their just powers from the consent of the governed, that whenever any form of government ~~shall~~ becomes destructive of these ends, it is the right of the people to alter or to abolish it, & to institute new government, laying it's foundation on such principles & organising it's powers in such form, as to them shall seem most likely to effect their safety & happiness. prudence indeed will dictate that governments long established should not be changed for light & transient causes: and accordingly all experience hath shewn that mankind are more disposed to suffer while evils are sufferable, than to right themselves by abolishing the forms to which they are accustomed. but when a long train of abuses & usurpations [begun at a distinguished period, &] pursuing invariably the same object evinces a design to ~~subject~~ reduce them to ~~arbitrary power~~ it is their right, it is their duty, to throw off such government & to provide new guards for their future security. such has been the patient sufferance of these colonies, & such is now the necessity which constrains them to [expunge] their former systems of government. the history of the present ~~king~~ king of Great Britain is a history of [unremitting] injuries and usurpations [among which, appears no solitary fact ~~to contra-~~ dict the uniform tenor of the rest [all of which] have]in direct object the establishment of an absolute tyranny over these states. to prove this let facts be submitted to a candid world. [for the truth of which we pledge a faith yet unsullied by falsehood]

he has refused his assent to laws the most wholesome and necessary for the public good:

he has forbidden his governors to pass laws of immediate & pressing importance,
unless suspended in their operation till his assent should be obtained;
and when so suspended, he has utterly neglected ~~utterly~~ to attend to them.

he has refused to pass other laws for the accomodation of large districts of people
unless those people would relinquish the right of representation in the legislature, a right
inestimable to them & formidable to tyrants only:

he has called together legislative bodies at places unusual, uncomfortable & distant from
the depository of their public records for the sole purpose of fatiguing them into compliance
with his measures;

he has dissolved Representative houses repeatedly [& continually] for opposing with
manly firmness his invasions on the rights of the people
~~[struck out]~~, he has refused for a long time after such dissolutions ~~space of time~~, to cause others to be elected;
whereby the legislative powers, incapable of annihilation, have returned to
the people at large for their exercise, the state remaining in the mean time
exposed to all the dangers of invasion from without & convulsions within

he has endeavored to prevent the population of these states; for that purpose
obstructing the laws for naturalization of foreigners, refusing to pass others
to encourage their migrations hither, & raising the conditions of new ap-
propriations of lands.

he has [suffered] obstructed the administration of justice [totally] to cease in some of these
states by refusing his assent to laws for establishing judiciary powers:

he has made [our] judges dependant on his will alone, for the tenure of their offices
and the amount & payment of their salaries
                                                                                                      † Dr. Franklin

he has erected a multitude of new offices [by a self-assumed power] & sent hi-
-ther swarms of officers to harrass our people & eat out their substance.

he has kept among us in times of peace, standing armies [& ships of war] without the consent of our legislature

he has affected to render the military independent of & superior to the civil power.

he has combined with others to subject us to a jurisdiction foreign to our constitu-
tions and unacknoleged by our laws; giving his assent to their acts of pretended ~~acts~~
& legislation, for quartering large bodies of armed troops among us;
for protecting them by a mock-trial from punishment for any murders
which they should commit on the inhabitants of these states,
for cutting off our trade with all parts of the world,
for imposing taxes on us without our consent:
for depriving us in many cases of the benefits of trial by jury

for transporting us beyond seas to be tried for pretended offences:
for abolishing the free system of English laws in a neighbouring province, establishing therein an arbitrary government
and enlarging it's boundaries so as to render it at once an example & fit instrument for introducing the same absolute
rule into these colonies [& states]

                                    valuable
abolishing our most ~~important~~ laws

for taking away our charters, ^altering fundamentally the forms of our governments

for suspending our own legislatures & declaring themselves invested with power to
legislate for us in all cases whatsoever:

he has abdicated government here, [withdrawing his governors, & declaring us out by declaring us out of his protection & waging war against us.
of his allegiance & protection:]

he has plundered our seas, ravaged our coasts, burnt our towns & destroyed the
lives of our people:

                                            Scotch and other
he is at this time transporting large armies of foreign mercenaries to compleat
the works of death, desolation & tyranny already begun with circumstances
                scarcely paralleled in the most barbarous ages, and totally
of cruelty & perfidy unworthy the head of a civilized nation:
he has ~~constrained our~~   excited domestic insurrections amongst us, and has
he has endeavored to bring on the inhabitants of our frontiers the merciless Indian
savages, whose known rule of warfare is an undistinguished destruction of
all ages, sexes, & conditions [of existence:]

[he has incited treasonable insurrections of our fellow-citizens, with the
allurements of forfeiture & confiscation of our property.
he has ~~constrained others~~
he has waged cruel war against human nature itself, violating it's most sa-
-cred rights of life & liberty in the persons of a distant people who never offended him, captivating & carrying them into slavery in another hemisphere, or to incur miserable death in their transportation thither. this
piratical warfare, the opprobrium of infidel powers, is the warfare of the
Christian king of Great Britain. determined to keep open a market
where MEN should be bought & sold: he has prostituted his negative
for suppressing every legislative attempt to prohibit or to restrain this
            ~~determining to keep open a market where MEN should be bought & sold:~~
execrable commerce: and that this assemblage of horrors might want no fact
of distinguished die, he is now exciting those very people to rise in arms
among us, and to purchase that liberty of which he has deprived them,
by murdering the people upon whom he also obtruded them. thus paying
off former crimes committed against the liberties of one people, with crimes
which he urges them to commit against the lives of another.]

in every stage of these oppressions we have petitioned for redress in the most humble
                                              only
terms; our repeated petitions have been answered by repeated injuries. a prince
whose character is thus marked by every act which may define a tyrant, is unfit
                                  are
to be the ruler of a people [who mean to be free: future ages will scarce believe
that the hardiness of one man, adventured within the short compass of twelve years
        to build a foundation so broad & undisguised, for tyranny
only ~~on so many acts of tyranny without a mask~~, over a people fostered & fixed in principle
of ~~liberty~~ freedom:]

Nor have we been wanting in attentions to our British brethren. we have warned them from time to time of attempts by their legislature to extend a jurisdiction over [these our states] we have reminded them of the circumstances of our emigration & settlement here, [no one of which could warrant so strange a pretension: that these were effected at the expence of our own blood & treasure, unassisted by the wealth or the strength of Great Britain: that in constituting indeed our several forms of government, we had adopted one common king, thereby laying a foundation for perpetual league & amity with them: but that submission to their parliament was no part of our constitution, nor ever in idea of history may be credited: and] we appealed to their native justice & magnanimity, [as well as to] the ties of our common kindred to disavow these usurpations which [were likely to] interrupt our correspondence & connection & they too have been deaf to the voice of justice & of consanguinity, [& when occasions have been given them by the regular course of their laws, of removing from their councils the disturbers of our harmony, they have by their free election re-established them in power. at this very time too they are permitting their chief magistrate to send over not only soldiers of our common blood, but Scotch & foreign mercenaries to invade & destroy us. these facts have given the last stab to agonising affection, and manly spirit bids us to renounce for ever these unfeeling brethren. we must endeavor to forget our former love for them, and to hold them as we hold the rest of mankind, enemies in war, in peace friends. we might have been a free & a great people together; but a communication of grandeur & of freedom it seems is below their dignity. be it so, since they will have it: the road to happiness & to glory is open to us too; we will tread it apart from them, and] acquiesce in the necessity which pronounces our [eternal] separation!

We therefore the representatives of the United States of America in General Congress assembled, do in the name & by authority of the good people of these [states,] [reject and renounce all allegiance & subjection to the kings of Great Britain & all others who may hereafter claim by, through, or under them; we utterly dissolve [& break off] all political connection which may heretofore have subsisted between us & the people or parliament of Great Britain; and finally we do assert and declare these colonies to be free and independant states, and that as free & independant states they have full power to levy war, conclude peace, contract alliances, establish commerce, & to do all other acts and things which independant states may of right do. And for the support of this declaration] we mutually pledge to each other our lives, our fortunes, & our sacred honour.

History Side Note: As soon as Congress approved the Declaration of Independence, the first signator, John Hancock mailed a copy of the Declaration of Independence to General George Washington. General Washington was at battle, he was the Commander-In-Chief, and Hancock rightly thought it was imperative for him to know that the American colonies had formally declared independence from Great Britain.

Philadelphia JULY 6th. 1776.

Sir,

The Congress, for some time past, have had their attention occupied by one of the most interesting and important subjects, that could possibly come before them or any other assembly of men.

Although it is not possible to foresee the consequences of human actions, yet it is, nevertheless, a duty we owe ourselves and posterity, in all our public councils, to decide in the best manner we are able, and to leave the event to that Being who controls both causes and events, to bring about his own determinations.

Impressed with this sentiment, and at the same time fully convinced that our affairs may take a more favorable turn, the Congress have judged it necessary to dissolve the connection between Great Britain and the American Colonies, and to declare them free and independent States, as you will perceive by the in closed DECLARATION, which I am directed by Congress to transmit to you, and to request you will have it proclaimed at the head of the army in the way you shall think most proper.

Agreeably to the request of Congress, the Committee of Safety of this Colony have forwarded to you ten thousand flints, and the Hints at Rhode Island are ordered to be sent to you immediately.

It is with great pleasure I inform you, that the militia of this Colony, of Delaware Government, and Maryland, are, and will be every day in motion, to form the Flying Camp, and that all the militia of this Colony will soon be in the Jerseys, ready to receive such orders as you shall please to give them.

I have written to Governor Cooke, to engage immediately, and send forward as fast as possible, fifty ship-carpenters to General Schuyler, for the purpose of building vessels on the Lakes. Fifty have already gone from hence on that business.

The Congress having directed the arms, taken on board the Scotch transports, to be sent to you. I have written to the agents in Rhode Island and Massachusetts Bay, to forward them immediately.

The inclosed copy of a letter from Mr. Green, I am directed to forward, by Congress, with a request that you will order such parts of the stores, therein mentioned, to New York, as you shall judge proper.

I have the honor to be, Sir, with perfect esteem, your most obedient and very humble servant,

JOHN HANCOCK, President

Towards Independence

Annotated from <u>Thomas Jefferson's Memoir, Correspondence and Miscellanies</u>. Written by Thomas Jefferson and edited by Thomas Jefferson Randolph. Gray and Bowen (Boston). G. & C. & H. Carvill) 1830.

Mr. Randolph was according to expectation obliged the chair of Congress, to attend the General Assembly summoned by **Lord Dunmore**, to meet on the 1st day of June, 1775. Lord North's conciliatory propositions, as they were called received by the Governor, and furnished the subject for which this assembly was convened. Mr. Randolph accordingly attended, and the tenor of these propositions being generally known, as having been addressed to all the governors, he was anxious that the answer of our Assembly, likely to be the first, should harmonise with what he knew to be the sentiments and wishes of the body he had recently left. He feared that Mr. Nicholas, whose mind was not yet up to the mark of the times, would undertake the answer, and therefore pressed me to prepare it. I did so, and, with his aid, carried it through the House, with long and doubtful scruples from Mr. Nicholas and James Mercer, and a dash of cold water on it here and there, enfeebling it somewhat, but finally with unanimity, or a vote approaching it. This being passed, I repaired immediately to Philadelphia, and conveyed to Congress the first notice they had of it. It was entirely approved there. I took my seat with them on the 21st of June. On the 24th, a committee which had been appointed to prepare a **declaration of the causes of taking up arms**, brought in their report (drawn, I believe, by J. Rutledge) which, not being liked, the House recommitted it, on the 26th, and added Mr. Dickinson and myself to the committee. On the rising of the House, the committee having not yet met, I happened to find myself near Governor W.

Livingston, and proposed to him to draw the paper. He excused himself and proposed that I should draw it. On my pressing him with urgency, 'We are as yet but new acquaintances, sir,' said he, 'why are you so earnest for my doing it?' 'Because,' said I, 'I have been informed that you drew the Address to the people of Great Britain, a production, certainly, of the finest pen in America.' 'On that,' says he, 'perhaps, sir, you may not have been correctly informed.' I had received the information in Virginia from Colonel Harrison on his return from that Congress. Lee, Livingston, and Jay had been the committee for the draught. The first, prepared by Lee, had been disapproved and recommitted. The second was drawn by Jay, but being presented by Governor Livingston, had led Colonel Harrison into the error. The next morning, walking in the hall of Congress, many members being assembled, but the House formed, I observed Mr. Jay speaking to R. H. Lee, and leading him by the button of his coat to me. 'I understand, sir,' said he to me, 'that this gentleman informed you, that Governor Livingston drew the Address to the people of Great Britain.' I assured him at once that I had not received that information from Mr. Lee and that not a word had ever passed on the subject between Mr. Lee and myself; and after some explanations the subject was dropped. These gentlemen had had some sparrings in debate before, and continued ever very hostile to each other.

I prepared a draught of the declaration committed to us. It was too strong for Mr. Dickinson. He still retained the hope of reconciliation with the mother country, and was unwilling it should be lessened by offensive statements. He was so honest a man, and so able a one, that he was greatly indulged even by those who could not feel his scruples. We therefore requested him to take the paper, and put it into a form he could approve. He did so, preparing an entire new statement, and preserving of the former only the last four paragraphs and half of the preceding one. We approved and reported it to Congress, who accepted it. Congress gave a signal proof of their indulgence to Mr. Dickinson, and of their great desire not to go too fast for any respectable part of our body, in permitting him to draw their second petition to the King according to his own ideas, and passing it with scarcely any amendment. The disgust against its humility was general; and Mr. Dickinson's delight at its passage was the only circumstance which reconciled them to it. The vote being passed, although further observation on it was out of order, he could not refrain from rising and expressing his satisfaction, and concluded by saying, 'There is but one word,

_____

_____

_____

_____

_____

_____

_____

_____

_____

_____

_____

_____

_____

_____

_____

_____

_____

Mr. President, in the paper which I disapprove, and that is the word Congress;' on which Ben Harrison rose and said, 'There is but one word in the paper, Mr. President, of which I approve, and that is the word Congress?'

On the 22nd of July, Dr. Franklin (*Benjamin Franklin*), Mr. Adams (*John Adams)*, R. H. Lee, and myself were appointed a committee to consider and report on Lord North's conciliatory resolution. The answer of the Virginia Assembly on that subject having been approved, I was requested by the committee to prepare this report, which will account for the similarity of feature in the two instruments.

On the 15th of May, 1776, the convention of Virginia instructed their delegates in Congress, to propose to that body to declare the colonies independent of Great Britain, and appointed a committee to prepare a declaration of rights and plan of government.

In Congress, Friday, June 7, 1776. The delegates from Virginia moved, in obedience to instructions from their constituents, that the Congress should declare that these United Colonies and of right ought to be, free and independent states, that they are absolved from all allegiance to the British crown, and that all political connection between them and the state of Great Britain is and ought to be, totally dissolved; that measures should be immediately taken for procuring the assistance of foreign powers and a confederation be formed to bind the colonial more closely together.

The House being obliged to attend at that time to some other business, the proposition was referred to the next day, when the members were ordered to attend punctually at ten o'clock.

Saturday, June 8. They proceeded to take it into consideration, and referred it to a committee of the whole, into which they immediately resolved themselves, and passed that day and Monday the 10th in debating on the subject.

It was argued by Wilson, Robert R. Livingston, E. Rutledge, Dickinson, and others—

That, though they were friends to the measures themselves, and saw the impossibility that we should ever again be united with Great Britain, yet they were against adopting them at this time:

That the conduct we had formerly observed was wise and proper now, of deferring to take any capital step till the voice of the people drove us into it:

That they were our power, and without them our declarations could not be carried into effect:

That the people of the middle colonies (Maryland, Delaware, Pennsylvania, the Jerseys, and New York) were not yet ripe for bidding adieu to British connection, but that they were fast ripening, and, in a short time, would join in the general voice of America:

That the resolution, entered into by this House on the 15th of May, for suppressing the exercise of all powers derived from the crown, had shown, by the ferment into which it had thrown these middle colonies, that they had not yet accommodated their minds to a separation from the mother country:

That some of them had expressly forbidden their delegates to consent to such a declaration, and others had given no instructions, and consequently no powers to give such consent:

That if the delegates of any particular colony had no power to declare such colony independent, certain they were, the others could not declare it for them; the colonies being as yet perfectly independent of each other:

That the assembly of Pennsylvania was now sitting above stairs, their convention would sit within a few days, the convention of New York was now sitting, and those of the Jerseys and Delaware counties would meet on the Monday following, and it was probable these bodies would take up the question of Independence, and would declare to their delegates the voice of their state:

That if such a declaration should now be agreed to, these delegates must retire, and possibly their colonies might secede from the Union:

That such a secession would weaken us more than could be compensated by any foreign alliance:

That in the event of such a division, foreign powers would either refuse to join themselves to our fortunes, or, having us so much in their power as that desperate declaration would place us, they would insist on terms proportionably more hard and prejudicial:

That we had little reason to expect an alliance with those to whom alone, as yet, we had cast our eyes:

That France and Spain had reason to be jealous of that

Jefferson puts forth an interesting point. He writes that some of the Congress urged an argument in support of the other side, of the British side, not because they opposed the separation from Great Britain, but because they did not see the need to declare something that already existed – their independence.

Use the reading to support the above argument:

Position: _____

_____

_____

Supporting Detail 1: _____

_____

_____

_____

Supporting Detail 2: _____

_____

_____

_____

Supporting Detail 3: _____

_____

_____

_____

Summary of idea: _____

_____

_____

_____

_____

_____

_____

_____

rising power, which would one day certainly strip them of all their American possessions:

That it was more likely they should form a connection with the British Court, who, if they should find themselves unable otherwise to extricate themselves from their difficulties, would agree to a partition of our territories, restoring Canada to France, and the Floridas to Spain, to accomplish for themselves a recovery of these colonies:

That it would not be long before we should receive certain information of the disposition of the French court, from the agent whom we had sent to Paris for that purpose:

That if this disposition should be favorable, by waiting the event of the present campaign, which we all hoped would be successful, we should have reason to expect an alliance on better terms:

That this would in fact work no delay of any effectual aid from such ally, as, from the advance of the season and distance of our situation, it was impossible we could receive any assistance during this campaign:

That it was prudent to fix among ourselves the terms on which we would form alliance, before we declared we would form one at all events:

And that if these were agreed on, and our Declaration of Independence ready by the time our Ambassador should be prepared to sail, it would be as well, as to go into that Declaration at this day.

On the other side, it was urged by J. Adams, Lee, Wythe and others, that no gentleman had argued against the policy or the right of separation from Britain, nor had supposed it possible we should ever renew our connection; that they had only opposed its being now declared:

That the question was not whether, by a Declaration of Independence, we should make ourselves what we are not; but whether we should declare a fact which already exists:

That, as to the people or parliament of England, we had always been independent of them, their restraints on our trade deriving efficacy from our acquiescence only, and not from any rights they possessed of imposing them, and that so far, our connection had been federal only, and was now dissolved by the commencement of hostilities:

That, as to the King, we had been bound to him by allegiance, but that this bond was now dissolved by his assent to the late act of parliament, by which he declares us out of his protection, and by his levying war on us, a fact which had long ago proved us out of his protection; it being a certain position in law, that allegiance and protection are reciprocal, the one ceasing when the other is withdrawn:

Other Continental Congress Debates regarding declaring independence put forth in Jefferson's Memoirs:

That James the II never declared the people of England out of his protection, yet his actions proved it and the parliament declared it:

No delegates that can be denied, or ever want, a power of declaring an existent truth:

That the delegates from the Delaware counties having declared their constituents ready to join, there are only two colonies, Pennsylvania and Maryland, whose delegates are absolutely tied up, and that these had, by their instructions, only reserved a right of confirming or rejecting the measure:

That the instructions from Pennsylvania might be accounted for from the times in which they were drawn, near a twelve month ago, since which the face of affairs has totally changed:

That within that time, it had become apparent that Britain was determined to accept nothing less than a *carte-blanche,* and that the King's answer to the Lord Mayor, Aldermen, and Common Council of London, which had come to hand four days ago, must have satisfied every one of this point:

That the people wait for us to lead the way:

That they are in favor of the measure, though the instructions given by some of their representatives are not:

That the voice of the representatives is not always consonant with the voice of the people, and that this is remarkably the case in these middle colonies:

That the effect of the resolution of the 15th of May has proved this, which, raising the murmurs of some in the colonies of Pennsylvania and Maryland, called forth the opposing voice of the freer part of the people, and proved them to be the majority even in these colonies:

That the backwardness of these two colonies might be ascribed, partly to the influence of proprietary power and connections, and partly, to their having not yet been attacked by the enemy:

That these causes were not likely to be soon removed, as there seemed no probability that the enemy would make either of these the seat of this summer's war:

That it would be vain to wait either weeks or months for perfect unanimity, since it was impossible that all men should ever become of one sentiment on any question:

That the conduct of some colonies, from the beginning of this contest, had given reason to suspect it was their settled policy to keep in the rear of the confederacy, that their particular prospect might be better, even in the worst event:

That, therefore, it was necessary for those colonies who had thrown themselves forward and hazarded all from the beginning, to come forward now also, and put all again to their own hazard:

That the history of the Dutch revolution, of whom three states only confederated at first, proved that a secession of some colonies would not be so dangerous as some apprehended:

That a declaration of Independence alone could render it consistent with European delicacy, for European powers to treat with us, or even to receive an Ambassador from us:

That till this, they would not receive our vessels into their ports, nor acknowledge the adjudications of our courts of admiralty to be legitimate, in cases of capture of British vessels:

That though France and Spain may be jealous of our rising power, they must think it will be much more formidable with the addition of Great Britain; and will therefore see it their interest to prevent a coalition; but should they refuse, we shall be but where we are; whereas without trying, we shall never know whether they will aid us or not:

That the present campaign may be unsuccessful, and therefore we had better propose an alliance while our affairs wear a hopeful aspect:

That to wait the event of this campaign will certainly work delay, because, during this summer, France may assist us effectually, by cutting off those supplies of provisions from England and Ireland, on which the enemy's armies here are to depend; or by setting in motion the great power they have collected in the West Indies, and calling our enemy to the defense of the possessions they have there:

That it would be idle to lose time in settling the terms of alliance, till we had first determined we would enter into alliance:

That it is necessary to lose no time in opening a trade for our people, who will want clothes, and will want money too, for the payment of taxes:

And that the only misfortune is, that we did not enter into alliance with France six months sooner, as, besides opening her ports for the vent of our last year's produce, she might have marched an army into Germany, and prevented the petty princes there, from selling their unhappy subjects to subdue us.

Activity: Choose at least one of the "debates" regarding declaring independence from Great Britain, research it on the internet and write:

Debate Chosen: _____

_____

_____

_____

What you think before conducting your research: _____

_____

_____

_____

_____

Summary of your research: _____

_____

_____

_____

_____

_____

_____

_____

_____

_____

_____

_____

_____

_____

_____

What you learned from your research: _____

_____

_____

_____

_____

_____

_____

_____

Your conclusions: _____

_____

_____

_____

_____

_____

_____

_____

_____

_____

_____

_____

_____

_____

_____

_____

_____

Describe the chain of events Jefferson puts forth on this and the next page.

_____

_____

_____

_____

_____

_____

_____

_____

_____

_____

_____

_____

_____

_____

_____

_____

_____

_____

_____

_____

_____

_____

_____

_____

_____

It appearing in the course of these debates, that the colonies of New York, New Jersey, Pennsylvania, Delaware, Maryland, and South Carolina were not yet matured for falling from the parent stem, but that they were fast advancing to that state, it was thought most prudent to wait awhile for them, and to postpone the final decision to July 1st: but, that this might occasion as little delay as possible, a committee was appointed to prepare a Declaration of Independence. The committee were John Adams, Dr. Franklin, Roger Sherman, Robert R. Livingston, and myself. Committees were also appointed, at the same time, to prepare a plan of confederation for the colonies, and to state the terms proper to be proposed for foreign alliance. The committee for drawing the Declaration of Independence desired me to do it. It was accordingly done, and being approved by them, I reported it to the House on Friday, the 28th of June, when it was read and ordered to lie on the table. On Monday, the 1st of July, the House resolved itself into a committee of the whole, and resumed the consideration of the original motion made by the delegates of Virginia, which, being again debated through the day, was carried in the affirmative by the votes of New Hampshire, Connecticut, Massachusetts, Rhode Island, New Jersey, Maryland, Virginia, North Carolina, and Georgia. South Carolina and Pennsylvania voted against it. Delaware had but two members present, and they were divided. The delegates from New York declared they were for it themselves, and were assured their constituents were for it; but that their instructions having been drawn near a twelvemonth before, when reconciliation was still the general object, they were enjoined by them to do nothing which should impede that object. They therefore thought themselves not justifiable in voting on either side, and asked leave to withdraw from the question; which was given them. The committee rose and reported their resolution to the House. Mr. Edward Rutledge, of South Carolina, then requested the determination might be put off to the next day, as he believed his colleagues, though they disapproved of the resolution, would then join in it for the sake of unanimity. The ultimate question, whether the House would agree to the resolution of the committee, was accordingly postponed to the next day, when it was again moved, and South Carolina concurred in voting for it. In the mean time, a third member had come post from the Delaware counties, and turned the vote of that colony in favor of the resolution. Members of a different sentiment attending that morning from Pennsylvania also, her vote was changed, so that the whole twelve colonies, who were authorized to vote at all, gave their voices for it; and, within a few days, [July 9.] the convention of New York approved of it, and thus supplied the void occasioned by the withdrawing of her delegates from the vote.

Congress proceeded the same day to consider the Declaration of Independence, which had been reported and laid on the table the Friday preceding, and on Monday referred to a committee of the whole. The pusillanimous idea that we had friends in England worth keeping terms with, still haunted the minds of many. For this reason, those passages which conveyed censures on the people of England were struck out, lest they should give them offence. The clause too, reprobating the enslaving the inhabitants of Africa, was struck out in complaisance to South Carolina and Georgia, who had never attempted to restrain the importation of slaves, and who, on the contrary, still wished to continue it. Our northern brethren also, I believe, felt a little tender under those censures; for though their people had very few slaves themselves, yet they had been pretty considerable carriers of them to others. The debates having taken up the greater parts of the 2nd, 3rd, and 4th days of July, were, on the evening of the last, closed; the Declaration was reported by the committee, agreed to by the House, and signed by every member present, except Mr. Dickinson. As the sentiments of men are known, not only by what they receive, but what they reject also, I will state the form of the Declaration as originally reported. The parts struck out by Congress shall be distinguished by a black line drawn under them; * and those inserted by them shall be placed in the margin, or in a concurrent column.

Document Analysis: Text from <u>Thomas Jefferson's Memoir, Correspondence and Miscellanies</u>

1. Type of Document: _____

2. Date of Document: _____ 3. Author of Document: _____

4. Title of the Document: _____

5. Who is the Document's Intended Audience: _____
_____
_____
_____

6. List three things the author said that you think are important:
_____
_____
_____

7. Why do you think the document was written:
_____
_____
_____

8. What is the evidence that helps you understand why it was written:
_____
_____
_____

9. List two things the document tells you about life in the United States at the time it was written:
_____
_____
_____

10. Write a question to the author that is left unanswered by the document:
_____
_____

11. Is the Document Biased: Why or why not?
_____
_____

Thomas Jefferson and Slavery

The writings of Thomas Jefferson are conflicted on the topic of slavery. Thomas Jefferson is famous as a foundation father, as a Revolutionary War author, as an inventor and as the President of the United States. He is the main author of the Declaration of Independence, he brokered the Louisiana Purchase, and he founded the University of Virginia. He even wrote a clause into the original Declaration of Independence denouncing slavery and yet he, himself, was a slave

RUN away from the subscriber in *Albemarle*, a Mulatto slave called *Sandy*, about 35 years of age, his stature is rather low, inclining to corpulence, and his complexion light; he is a shoemaker by trade, in which he uses his left hand principally, can do coarse carpenters work, and is something of a horse jockey; he is greatly addicted to drink, and when drunk is insolent and disorderly, in his conversation he swears much, and in his behaviour is artful and knavish. He took with him a white horse, much scarred with traces, of which it is expected he will endeavour to dispose; he also carried his shoemakers tools, and will probably endeavour to get employment that way. Whoever conveys the said slave to me, in *Albemarle*, shall have 40 s. reward, if taken up within the county, 4 l. if elsewhere within the colony, and 10 l. if in any other colony, from
THOMAS JEFFERSON.

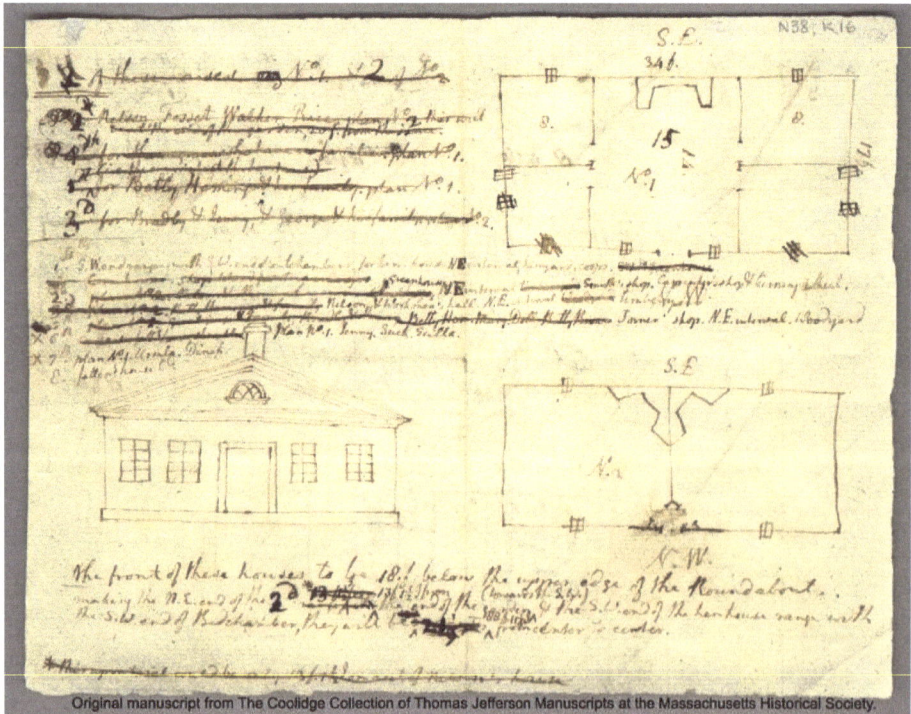

owner. The advertisement, at right, published in *The Virginia Gazette* (Williamsburg), on September 14, 1769, is a notice from Jefferson regarding a runaway slave.

He owned slaves, yet, Jefferson called slavery an "abominable crime". He aided in outlawing the international slave trade to Virginia. He considered slavery a moral travesty and evil beyond reproach; however, he owned several hundred slaves at his home in Monticello.

Original manuscript from The Coolidge Collection of Thomas Jefferson Manuscripts at the Massachusetts Historical Society.

In correspondence to friends and associates Jefferson denounces slavery sometimes, yet at other times he is purposely ambiguous and still other times his letters and writings indicate he was adamantly against slavery, but then he continues to profess that it must continue. Jefferson's relationship with slavery is rife with contradiction. In reading the following, please keep the question in mind: **Where did Thomas stand on the issue of slavery?**

Slavery: Thomas Jefferson was born in 1743. Slavery had been in existence in the colonies for decades. Slavery had been in existence in Virginia for approximately seventy-five years. Jefferson grew up on a plantation. He grew up knowing only the slave culture. As an adult, Jefferson owned 200 slaves at one time. Early on, it is evident that Jefferson viewed African slaves as inferior.

Benjamin Banneker, to whom the letter is addressed, was an African-American mathematician and publisher of a popular almanac stating that both no matter what a person's color their relationship to God is the same – thus then they are they are the same and should be treated as such under God.

Philadelphia Aug. 30. 1791.

Sir,

I thank you sincerely for your letter of the 19th. instant and for the Almanac it contained. no body wishes more than I do to see such proofs as you exhibit, that nature has given to our black brethren, talents equal to those of the other colours of men, & that the appearance of a want of them is owing merely to the degraded condition of their existence both in Africa & America. I can add with truth that no body wishes more ardently to see a good system commenced for raising the condition both of their body & mind to what it ought to be, as fast as the imbecillity of their present existence, and other circumstance which cannot be neglected, will admit. I have taken the liberty of sending your almanac to Monsieur de Condorcet, Secretary of the Academy of sciences at Paris, and member of the Philanthropic society because I considered it as a document to which your whole colour had a right for their justification against the doubts which have been entertained of them. I am with great esteem, Sir, Your most obedt. humble servt. Th. Jefferson

---

Re-write the above letter in your own words:

_____

_____

_____

_____

_____

_____

_____

_____

_____

_____

_____

_____

_____

_____

451

a very worthy & respectable member of society. he is a free man. I shall be delighted to see these instances of moral eminence so multiplied as to prove that the want of talents observed in them is merely the effect of their degraded condition, and not proceeding from any difference in the structure of the parts on which intellect depends.

I am looking ardently to the completion of the glorious work in which your country is engaged. I view the general condition of Europe as hanging on the success or failure of France. having set such an example of philosophical arrangement within, I hope it will be extended without your limits also, and to your dependants and to your friends in every part of the earth.

Present my affectionate respects to Madame de Condorcet, and accept yourself assurance of the sentiment of esteem & attachment with which I have the honour to be Dear Sir

your most obedt

& most humble servt

Th: Jefferson.

V. V.
11178   62-96

The Marquis de Condorcet was a famous French mathematician and abolitionist and Jefferson's letter above (copy from the Library of Congress) seems to indicate that Jefferson thought highly of Banneker; however, on his Banneker's death, Jefferson expressed the opinion that he believed Banneker may have received help from someone else when writing his almanacs.

Monticello, October 8, 1809

Dear Sir,

—It is long since I ought to have acknowledged the receipt of your most excellent oration on the 4th of July. I was doubting what you could say, equal to your own reputation on so hackneyed a subject; but you have really risen out of it with lustre, and pointed to others a field of great expansion. A day or two after I received your letter to Bishop Gregoire, a copy of his diatribe to you came to hand from France. I had not before heard of it. He must have been eagle-eyed in quest of offence, to have discovered ground for it among the rubbish massed together in the print he animadverts on. You have done right in giving him a sugary answer. But he did not deserve it. For, notwithstanding a compliment to you now and then, he constantly returns to the identification of your sentiments with the extravagances of the Revolutionary zealots. I believe him a very good man, with imagination enough to declaim eloquently, but without judgment to decide. He wrote to me also on the doubts I had expressed five or six and twenty years ago, in the *Notes of Virginia,* as to the grade of understanding of the negroes, and he sent me his book on the literature of the negroes. His credulity has made him gather up every story he could find of men of color, (without distinguishing whether black, or of what degree of mixture,) however slight the mention, or light the authority on which they are quoted. The whole do not amount, in point of evidence, to what we know ourselves of Banneker. We know he had spherical trigonometry enough to make almanacs, but not without the suspicion of aid from Ellicot, who was his neighbor and friend, and never missed an opportunity of puffing him. I have a long letter from Banneker, which shows him to have had a mind of very common stature indeed. As to Bishop Gregoire, I wrote him, as you have done, a very soft answer. It was impossible for doubt to have been more tenderly or hesitatingly expressed than that was in the *Notes of Virginia,* and nothing was or is farther from my intentions, than to enlist myself as the champion of a fixed opinion, where I have only expressed a doubt. St. Domingo will, in time, throw light on the question.

I intended, ere this, to have sent you the papers I had promised you. But I have taken up Marshall's fifth volume, and mean to read it carefully, to correct what is wrong in it, and commit to writing such facts and annotations as the reading of that work will bring into my recollection, and which has not yet been put on paper; in this I shall be much aided by my memorandums and letters, and will send you both the old and the new.[1] But I go on very slowly. In truth, during the pleasant season, I am always out of doors, employed, not passing more time at my writing table than will despatch my current business. But when the weather becomes cold, I shall go out but little. I hope, therefore, to get through this volume during the ensuing winter; but should you want the papers sooner, they shall be sent at a moment's warning. The ride from Washington to Monticello in the stage, or in a gig, is so easy that I had hoped you would have taken a flight here during the season of good roads. Whenever Mrs. Barlow is well enough to join you in such a visit, it must be taken more at ease. It will give us real pleasure whenever it may take place. I pray you to present me to her respectfully, and I salute you affectionately.

Text of actual letter

A Letter From Thomas Jefferson to John Holmes, Discussing slavery and the Missouri question.

TO GENERAL CHASTELLUX.
Paris, June 7, 1785
Dear Sir,

I have been honored with the receipt of your letter of the 2nd instant, and am to thank you, as I do sincerely, for the partiality with which you receive the copy of the Notes on my country. As I can answer for the facts therein reported on my own observation, and have admitted none on the report of others, which were not supported by evidence sufficient to command my own assent, I am not afraid that you should make any extracts you please for the Journal de Physique, which come within their plan of publication. The strictures on slavery and on the constitution of Virginia, are not of that kind, and they are the parts which I do not wish to have made public, at least, till I know whether their publication would do most harm or good. It is possible, that in my own country, these strictures might produce an irritation, which would indispose the people towards the two great objects I have in view, that is, the emancipation of their slaves, and the settlement of their constitution on a firmer and more permanent basis. If I learn from thence, that they will not produce that effect, I have printed and reserved just copies enough to be able to give one to every young man at the College. It is to them I look, to the rising generation, and not to the one now in power, for these great reformations. The other copy, delivered at your hotel, was for Monsieur de Buffon. I meant to ask the favor of you to have it sent to him, as I was ignorant how to do it. I have one also for Monsieur Daubenton, but being utterly unknown to him, I cannot take the liberty of presenting it, till I can do it through some common acquaintance.

I will beg leave to say here a few words on the general question of the degeneracy of animals in America. 1. As to the degeneracy of the man of Europe transplanted to America, it is no part of Monsieur de Buffon's system. He goes, indeed, within one step of it, but he stops there. The Abbe Raynal alone has taken that step. Your knowledge of America enables you to judge this question; to say, whether the lower class of people in America, are less informed, and less susceptible of information, than the lower class in Europe: and whether those in America who have received such an education as that country can give, are less improved by it than Europeans of the same degree of education. 2. As to the aboriginal man of America, I know of no respectable evidence on which the opinion of his inferiority of genius has been founded, but that of Don Ulloa. As to Robertson, he never was in America; he relates nothing on his own knowledge; he is a compiler only of the relations of others, and a mere translator of the opinions of Monsieur de Buffon. I should as soon, therefore, add the translators of Robertson to the witnesses of this fact, as himself. Paw, the beginner of this charge, was a compiler from the works of others; and of the most unlucky description; for he seems to have read the writings of travellers, only to collect and republish their lies. It is really remarkable, that in three volumes 12mo, of small print, it is scarcely possible to find one truth, and yet, that the author should be able to produce authority for every fact he states, as he says he can. Don Ulloa's testimony is of the most respectable. He wrote of what he saw, but he saw the Indian of South America only, and that, after he had passed through ten generations of slavery. It is very unfair, from this sample, to judge of the natural genius of this race of men; and after supposing that Don Ulloa had not sufficiently calculated the allowance which should be made for this circumstance, we do him no injury in considering the picture he draws of the present Indians of South America, as no picture of what their ancestors were, three hundred years ago. It is in North America we are to seek their original character. And I am safe in affirming that the proofs of genius given by the Indians of North America, place them on a level with whites in the same uncultivated state. The North of Europe furnishes subjects enough for comparison with them, and for a proof of their equality. I have seen some thousands myself, and conversed much with them, and have found in them a masculine, sound understanding. I have had much information from men who had lived among them, and whose veracity and good sense were so far known to me, as to establish a reliance on their information. They have all agreed in bearing witness in favor of the genius of this a people. As to their bodily strength, their manners rendering it disgraceful to labor, those muscles employed in labor will be weaker with them, than with the European laborer; but those which are exerted in the chase, and those faculties which are employed in the tracing an enemy or a wild beast, in contriving ambuscades for him, and in carrying them through their execution, are much stronger than with us, because they are more exercised. I believe the Indian, then, to be, in body and mind, equal to the white man. I have supposed the black man, in his present state, might not be so; but it would be hazardous to affirm, that, equally cultivated for a few generations, he would not become so. 3. As to the inferiority of the other animals of America, without more facts, I can add nothing to what I have said in my Notes.

As to the theory of Monsieur de Buffon, that heat is friendly, and moisture adverse to the production of large animals, I am lately furnished with a fact by Benjamin Franklin, which proves the air of London and of Paris to be more humid than that of Philadelphia and so creates a suspicion that the opinion of the superior humidity of America, may, perhaps, have been too hastily adopted. And supposing that fact admitted, I think the physical reasonings urged to show, that in a moist country animals must be small, and that in a hot one they must be large, are not built on the basis of experiment. These questions, however, cannot be decided ultimately, at this day. More facts must be collected, and more time flow off, before the world will be ripe for decision. In the mean time, doubt is wisdom.

I have been fully sensible of the anxieties of your situation, and that your attentions were wholly consecrated, where alone they were wholly due, to the succor of friendship and worth. However much I prize your society, I wait with patience the moment when I can have it without taking what is due to another. In the mean time, I am solaced with the hope of possessing your friendship, and that it is not ungrateful to you to receive the assurances of that with which I have the honor to be,

Dear Sir, your most obedien and most humble servant, Th Jefferson

Document Analysis: Text from <u>Thomas Jefferson's Memoir, Correspondence and Miscellanies</u>

1. Type of Document: _____

2. Date of Document: _____ 3. Author of Document: _____

4. Title of the Document: _____

5. Who is the Document's Intended Audience: _____
_____
_____
_____

6. List three things the author said that you think are important:
_____
_____
_____

7. Why do you think the document was written:
_____
_____
_____

8. What is the evidence that helps you understand why it was written:
_____
_____
_____

9. List two things the document tells you about life in the United States at the time it was written:
_____
_____
_____

10. Write a question to the author that is left unanswered by the document:
_____
_____

11. Is the Document Biased? Why or why not?
_____
_____

Document Analysis:

1. Did Thomas Jefferson believe slaves were people?

_____

_____

_____

_____

_____

_____

_____

2. Jefferson writes: **"Justice is in one scale, and self-preservation in the other…"** what does he mean?

_____

_____

_____

_____

_____

_____

_____

3. Describe how Jefferson feels about the future of the business of slavery.

_____

_____

_____

_____

_____

_____

_____

Think and Write: What do You Think

Please consider and answer the following question: What was Thomas Jefferson's opinion of slavery?

I think Thomas Jefferson's opinion of slavery was…
I think this because…
Documents that support my opinion include…
Detail to support my opinion…
Evidence supporting my detail…
Detail to support my opinion…
Evidence supporting my detail…
Detail to support my opinion…
Evidence supporting my detail…

Acknowledgments

Page 8: photo of Declaration Draft: Library of Congress

Page 9-10: Letter to Henry Lee: Library of Congress

Page 13: Little Journeys To the Homes of the Great *Volume 3, Little Journeys to the Homes of American Statesmen* by Elbert Hubbard. Originally published in 1916

Page 15: Photo of Wren Building at College of William and Mary © 2013 Lucky Jenny Publishing

Page 15: Photo of Virginia House of Burgesses © 2013 Lucky Jenny Publishing

Pages 32-35: Copy of Draft of Declaration of Independence: U.S. National Archives

Pages 37-46: Annotated from Thomas Jefferson's Memoir, Correspondence and Miscellanies. Edited by Thomas Jefferson Randolph. Gray and Bowen (Boston). G. & C. & H. Carvill) 1830.

Page 48: Picture of Slave Advertisement, The Virginia Gazette: University of Virginia online

Page 48: Monticello: stone house (slave quarters), recto, September 1770, by Thomas Jefferson. N38; K16 [electronic edition]. *Thomas Jefferson Papers: An Electronic Archive.* Boston, Mass. : Massachusetts Historical Society, 2003. http://www.thomasjeffersonpapers.org/

Page 50: Banneker correspondences: Library of Congress

Notes on Answers: The majority of student responses for this text require critical thinking on the part of students and should not be considered wrong unless it is evident that the document was not even read. Critical thinking and idea crafting should be encouraged. Working in groups or pairs should also be encouraged; however, student should arrive at their own opinions and draft their own ideas on paper.

The active reading side boxes for the passages are designed to help student's understand the text. It is helpful to demonstrate and model active reading techniques for students who may be unfamiliar with the process. Reading a page or two with students and modeling how to read critically will allow you to show students how to read for information and how to analyze non-fiction text.

The paragraphs and constructed response answers will vary. Please check that students support their assertions and stress that complete sentences and correct spelling and grammar will be considered. Again, as long as student thinking is supported by evidence – it is correct.

Document Analysis page 1

(1) Letter (2) May 8, 1825 (3) Thomas Jefferson

(4) To Henry Lee, Monticello, May 8, 1825

(5) The audience was Henry Lee (6) 1. Jefferson mentioned the sources he considered important for ideas contained in the Declaration of Independence – Locke, Cicero and Aristotle. 2. That the writing of the Declaration of Independence was to find something new or never thought of but to lay out the common sense of the freedoms entitled to men. 3. The Declaration was intended to communicate what the Americans thought. (7) Why do you think the document was written: The letter was written to a friend and fellow statesmen. First, Jefferson talks about what appears to be a donation to the University. Lee apparently mentioned, in his letter, something about notes of George Mason, who helped frame the Constitution and the Bill of Rights. I think Jefferson was trying to get the point across that object of the Declaration were/are simple. Jefferson seems to be defending the "Whigs" as being unified and all in agreement. He also seems to be pointing out that what he and the other colonists were doing was not something unheard of or never before done, but based on the thoughts and writings of great thinkers of liberty and ideas around a republic. (8) What is the evidence that helps you understand why is was written: The date it was written – some 50 years after the Declaration. Perhaps he was trying to restate ideas. He also says that the authority of the document does not belong to him or his peers, but to the "harmonizing sentiments of the day".

(9) List two things the document tells you about life in the United States at the time it was written: That even back when Jefferson was alive schools had to be careful what they spent money on because there wasn't apparently wasn't a lot then either. Jefferson opens the letter discussing a donation and the procurement of objects. He then states that the head of the department in questions thinks their collection is large enough and implies that money is an issue. Secondly, it tells me that Jefferson didn't think there was anything earth-shattering about the Declaration, but seemed to view it as a restatement of what ought to be the rights of men. That you can even look in elementary books of the great philosophers and discover the Declaration.

10. Write a question to the author that is left unanswered by the document: Mr. Jefferson, how is it you believe that nothing new is written in the Declaration of Independence when you included, in a culture of slavery, "all men are created equal". Who did you mean by all? Or, that in colonies that were separate and nowhere near states, how could you declare the purpose of a government to protect the natural rights of its people?

Page 14:

Physical features: tall, red-hair, freckles, white, pointed chin, pointed nose

Intellect: smart

Family: His father was dead and his mother was weak and an invalid. He also has sisters

Page 14 Summary: The College of William and Mary was founded in 1692 for the purpose of Christianizing natives and teaching religion. Thomas Jefferson was 14-years old when he entered the college. He was not sent to college, but went there on his own after his father died. It was the last dying wish of Thomas Jefferson's father that Thomas be educated, so he went to fulfill his father's wish.

Page 24 Document Analysis:

(1) Letter (2) August 25, 1775 (3) Thomas Jefferson (4) To John Randolph, August 25, 1775 (5) A friend and cousin to Thomas Jefferson and a loyalist that left for Great Britain in the very early days of the American Revolution (6) The author hopes to return to the days before the conflict and have his rights restored by Great Britain, that Jefferson would rather be dependent on Britain than any other nation so long as the colonies are not legislated by them, and he hopes his friend (who is heading back to Great Britain) will help to speed up the process of Great Britain ending the taxation and other laws they imposed. (7) I think the document was written as a farewell from Jefferson to Randolph and a gentle request from Jefferson to ask Randolph to use any political clout he has in Great Britain to help them understand that the colonists are serious, strong and carry their cause to the end. It appears that Jefferson would also like his friend help influence the government in Great Britain to back off so the colonies can go back to being peacefully loyal and basically left alone. (8) The evidence that helps me to decide this is the date it was written as well as the fact that Jefferson states that he will miss his friend and hopes he will help the British understand the situation and hastily resolve to go back to the way things were. (9) This document tells me that the colonists, or at least those in Jefferson's circle were calculated and had faith that they could be victorious in defending their cause. It also tells me that Jefferson was, at least in part, loyal to the crown and was only after what was right and fair. He wasn't looking for a fight, nor was secession his true goal but really his belief that all men are created equal and that they were entitled to basic rights. (10) In the letter, Jefferson alludes that he would like things to work out, end peacefully and go back to the way things were; however, I wonder if that is how he really felt. I would like to know the conflict he felt and if he ever questioned moving forward and declaring independence.

Page 26: Document Analysis:

(1) Letter (2) November 29, 1775 (3) Thomas Jefferson (4) To John Randolph, November 29, 1775 (5) A friend and cousin of Thomas Jefferson's and a loyalist who returned to Great Britain (6) That Lord Dunmore has begun hostilities in Virginia, they have hope that the delegates in Canada will take up with the cause and that Lord Dunmore tried to burn down the town of Hampton, but did not succeed. (7) To inform Randolph that a colleague has died. Plus, the document seems to be written to inform his friend and cousin of the situation in America and tell him that Jefferson doesn't want a separation but is willing to continue to fight for one. He also seems to be implying that it is close to a time when going back may not be possible. (8) The evidence that helps me understand why it was written includes the tone of the letter and the fact that the first sentence is information about the passing of the friend and the rest has a strong emphasis on how well the colonists are doing and how they intend to get their way. (9) The document tells me that the colonists are confident in their ability to beat the British and that the Governor appointed by the British is failing. (10) I would like to ask Jefferson if he really thought the conflict would end quickly.

Page 28: Document Analysis:

(1) Letter (2) August 13, 1777 (3) Thomas Jefferson (4) To Benjamin Franklin, August 13, 1777 (5) Fellow founding father Benjamin Franklin (6) That it seemed to surprise Jefferson how easy Virginia traded the monarchy for a republic form of government, that the new country need to either close their ports and manufacture their own goods or to figure out a way to trade, and that some continue to try to hold on to their sovereignty. (7) To inform Benjamin Franklin of the happenings in Virginia and tell Franklin that he wished it possible to be like Franklin and reside in polite Court. (8) It is more matter of fact that the previous two letters and Franklin is away. (9) That people so easily let go of the British Government and that there seems to be a "quiet exercise of government". By the tone of the letter it seems that life is peaceful in Virginia or relatively so. (10) Did the transition of the government really go as smoothly as this letter implies and was life for the ordinary citizen any different during the American Revolution than during the time before the war.

Page 28: Question: The links between the three documents include: Jefferson's confidence in America and the colonists getting their way one way or another and/or that Jefferson really doesn't harbor ill-will toward the British – that he just wants the colonists to have the rights they deserve. Other links may be accepted if they are backed with evidence from the letters.

Pages 30 and 31 are Think and Writes: There are no wrong answers provided student answers are supported by details from the writings that are substantiated.

Page 43: Answers will vary depending upon which debate is chosen.

Page 48: Answers will vary.

Page 51: (1) Jefferson refers to slaves as human beings at various points of the passage. He also implies that they should not be labeled as property. I think that the line "…of one thing I am certain, that as the passage of slaves from one state to another would not make a slave of a single human being who would not be so without it, so their diffusion over a greater surface would make them individually happier and proportionally facilitate the accomplishment of their emancipation" illustrates that Jefferson considered all people human until they are enslaved and that he considered slaves property. The letter is very conflicted. (2) That it is more just to free

www.ingramcontent.com/pod-product-compliance
Lightning Source LLC
LaVergne TN
LVHW072107070426
835509LV00002B/46